PIANO / VOCAL / GUITAR

the twilight saga
eclipse

MUSIC FROM THE
MOTION PICTURE SOUNDTRACK

ISBN 978-1-4234-9789-9

HAL•LEONARD
CORPORATION

7777 W. BLUEMOUND RD. P.O. BOX 13819 MILWAUKEE, WI 53213

Visit Hal Leonard Online at
www.halleonard.com

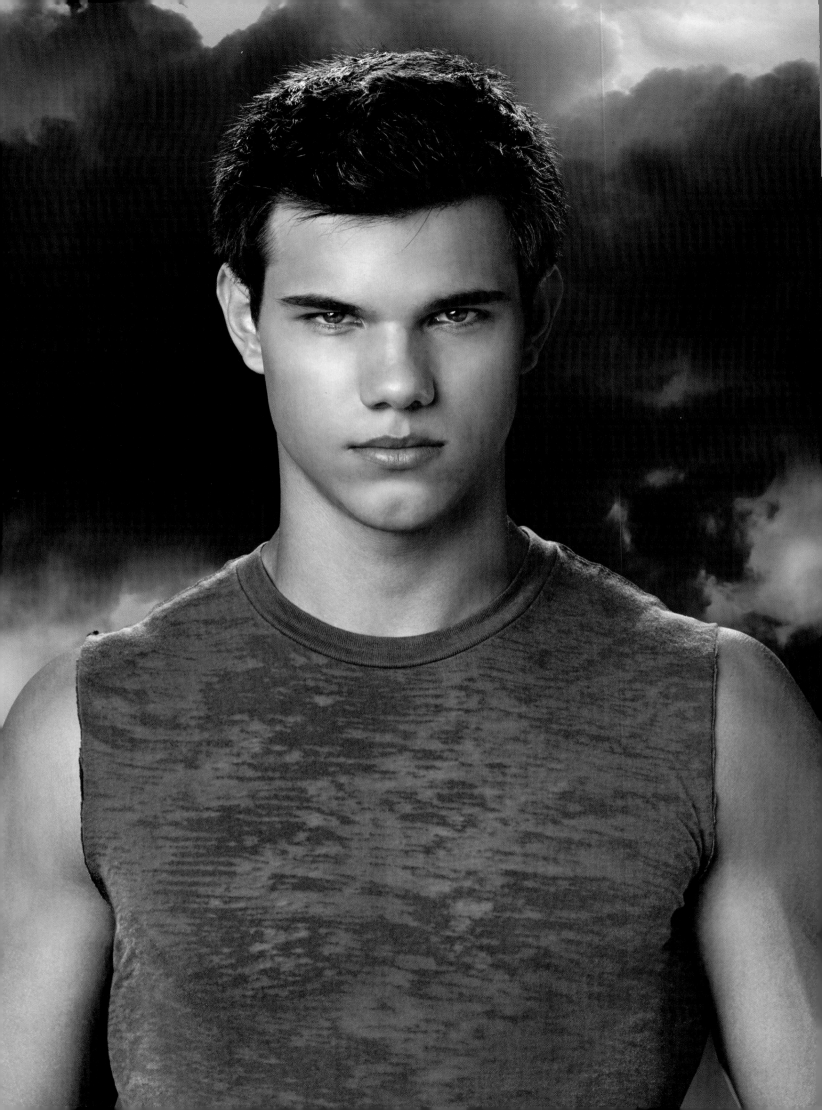

ECLIPSE (ALL YOURS)

Written by EMILY HAINES,
JAMES SHAW and HOWARD SHORE

NEUTRON STAR COLLISION
(Love Is Forever)

Words and Music by
MATTHEW BELLAMY

Slow Ballad

I was search-ing, you were on a ___ mis-sion.

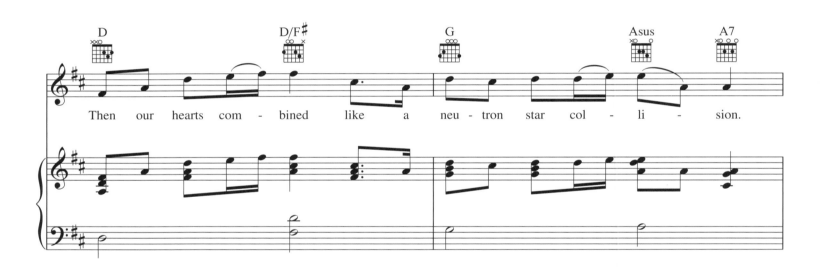

Then our hearts com-bined like a neu-tron star col-li-sion.

I had noth-ing left to lose, you took your time to

* Recorded a half step lower.

OURS

Words and Music by DAN WILSON
and SAMUEL ENDICOTT

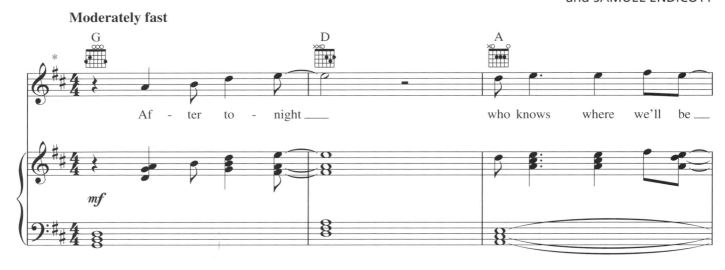

After to-night ___ who knows where we'll be ___

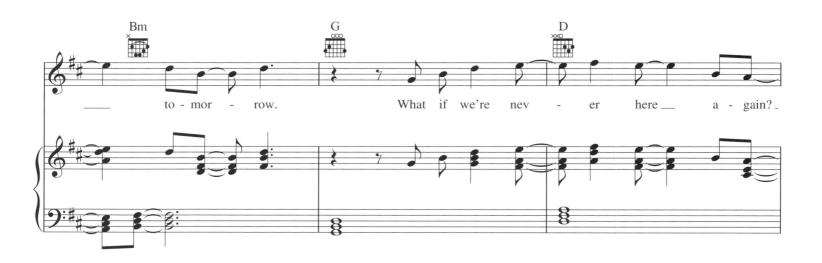

___ to-mor-row. What if we're nev-er here ___ a-gain? ___

Driving New Wave Rock

Af-ter to-night ___

* *Recorded a half step lower.*

HEAVY IN YOUR ARMS

Words and Music by FLORENCE WELCH
and PAUL EPWORTH

MY LOVE

Words and Music by SIA FURLER
and OLIVER KRAUS

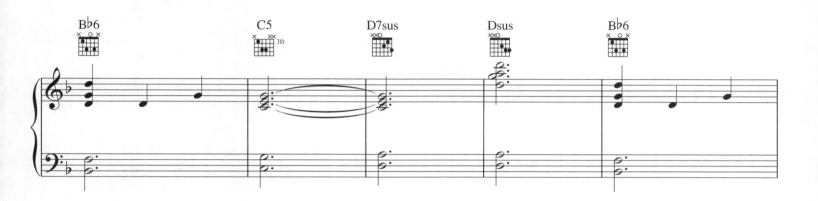

ATLAS

Words and Music by
FANFARLO

Quick Country Folk feel

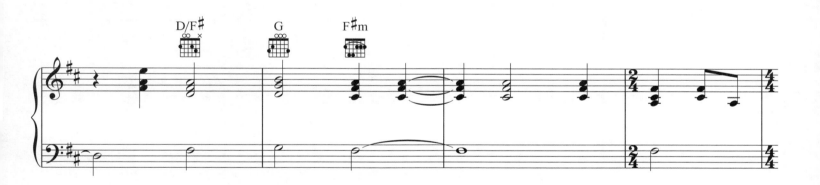

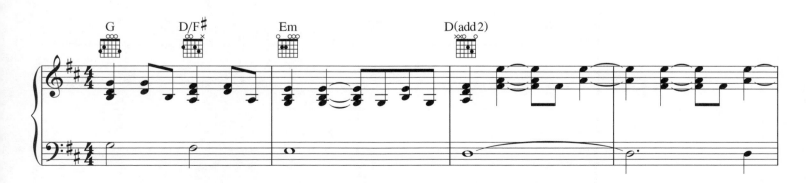

44

CHOP AND CHANGE

Words and Music by DAN AUERBACH
and PATRICK CARNEY

48

ROLLING IN ON A BURNING TIRE

Words and Music by ALISON MOSSHART,
DEAN FERTITA, JACK LAWRENCE
and JACK WHITE

The moon is al-ways full for us; the road is al-ways clear. But that's not what you want to hear.

That's not what you want to hear.

LET'S GET LOST

Words and Music by NATASHA KHAN
and BECK HANSEN

let's   get   lost.

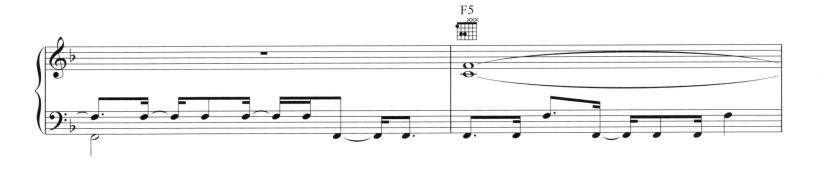

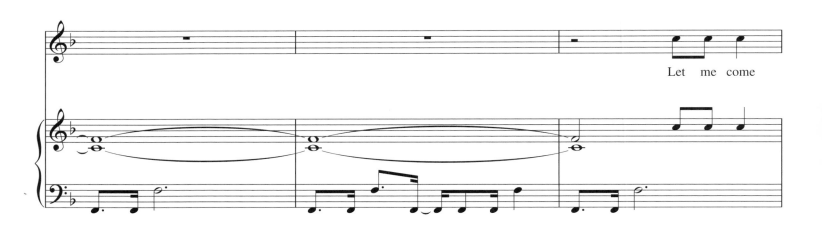

Let   me   come

night, dar - ling, let's get lost.

If just for to - night, _____ dar - ling, _____

let's get lost.

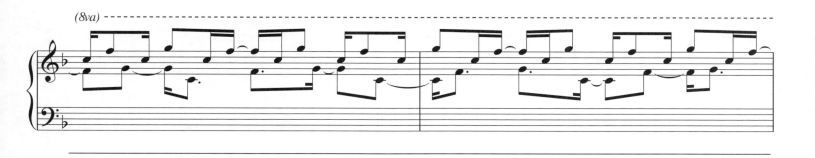

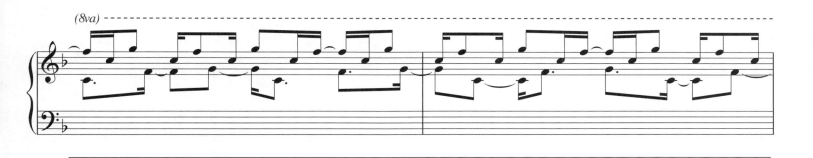

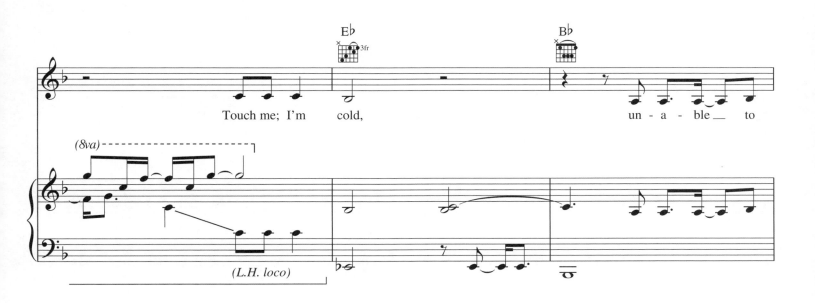

Touch me; I'm cold,

un - a - ble __ to

JONATHAN LOW

Lyrics by EZRA KOENIG
Music by CHRIS BAIO, ROSTAM BATMANGLIJ,
EZRA KOENIG and CHRISTOPHER TOMSON

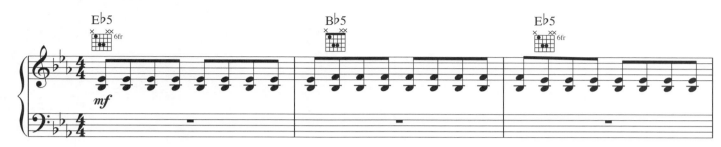

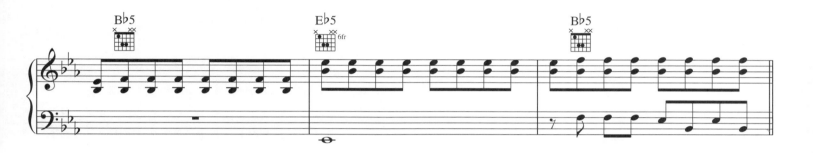

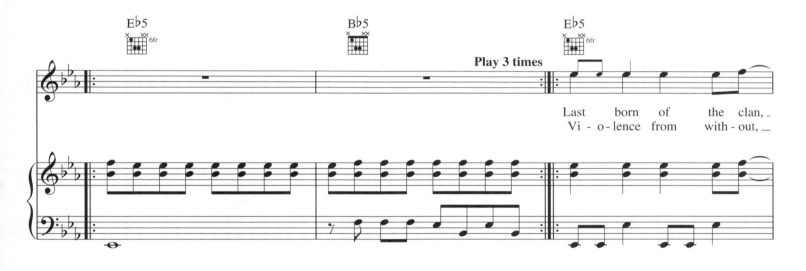

Last born of the clan,
Vi - o - lence from with - out, __

first one to be free, __
and an - ger from with - in. __

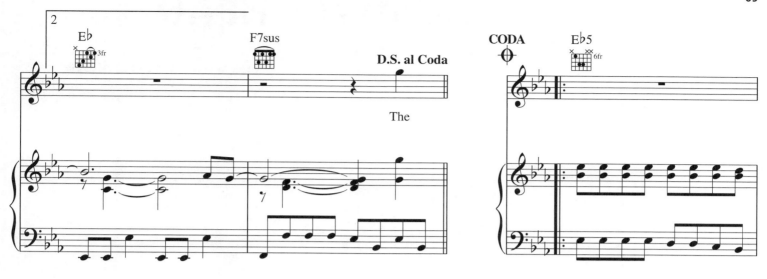

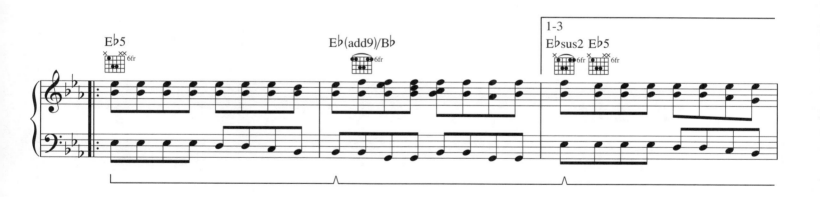

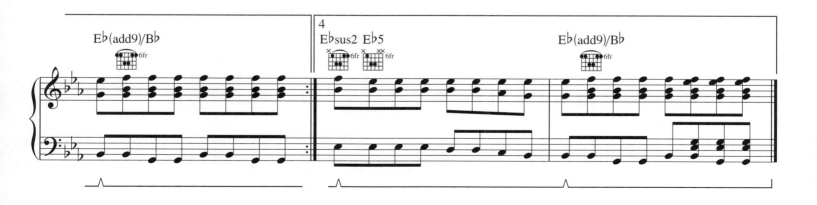

WITH YOU IN MY HEAD

Words and Music by ALEXANDER MAAS,
JAMES LAVELLE, PABLO CLEMENTS
and JAMES GRIFFITH

Singin' in tongues, it makes me sum-mon.
(Sing-in' in tongues, it makes me sum-mon.)

Al-most there, I'm read-y, hon-ey. I got all those

cares you gave me, and all that I ev-er

A MILLION MILES AN HOUR

Words and Music by JOSH OSTRANDER,
MELISSA DOUGHERTY and GREG LYONS

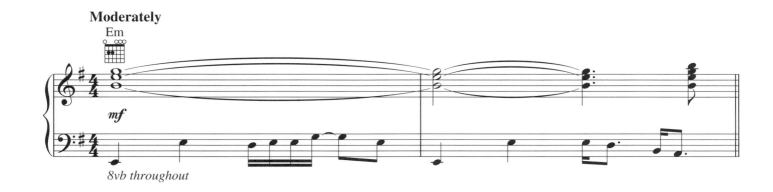

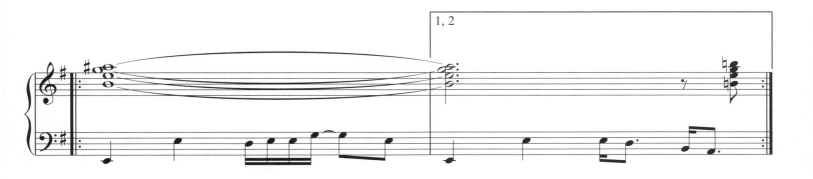

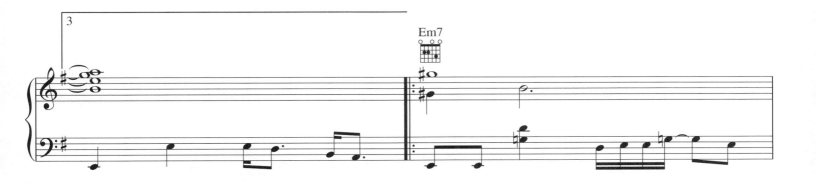

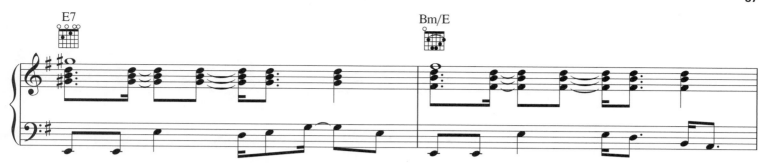

I can go ___ a mil - lion miles ___ an hour. ___

LIFE ON EARTH

Words and Music by BENJAMIN BRIDWELL,
CREIGHTON BARRETT, BILL REYNOLDS,
TYLER RAMSEY and RYAN MONROE

To Coda ⊕

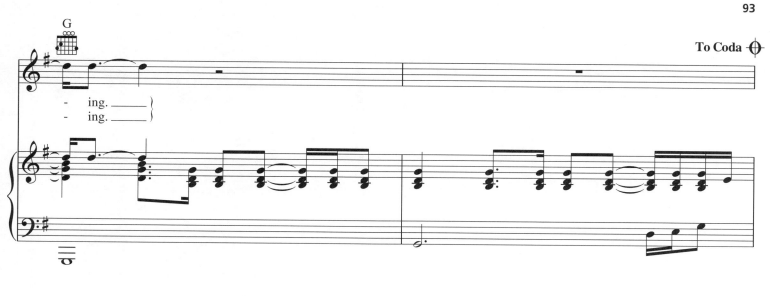

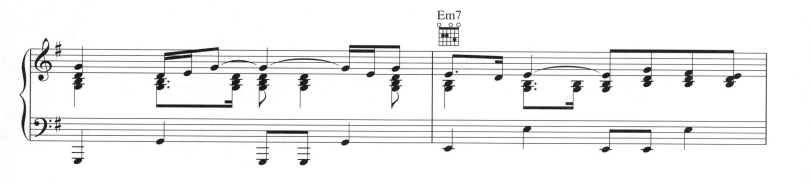

WHAT PART OF FOREVER

Words and Music by THOMAS CALLAWAY,
OH, HUSH! and ROBERT KLEINER

Moderately fast

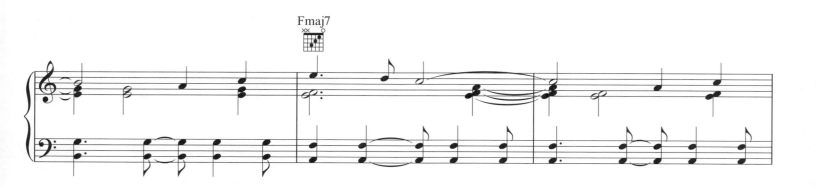

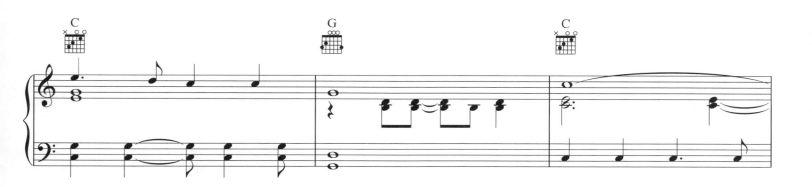

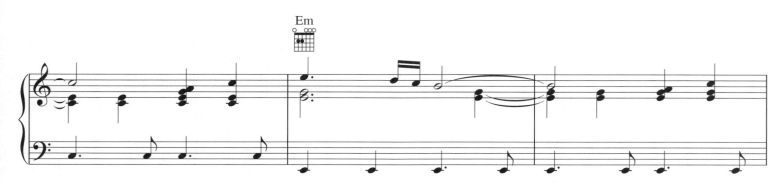

(I'll give it to you.) —

1
(I had a heart.)

2
(I had a heart.) —

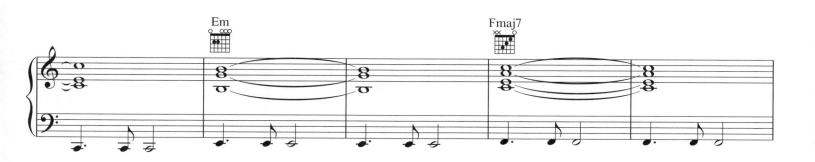

Repeat ad lib. and Fade

Optional Ending

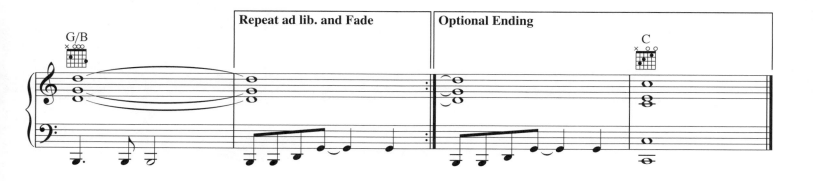

JACOB'S THEME

Composed by
HOWARD SHORE

THE LINE

Words and Music by TYONDAI BRAXTON,
DAVID KONOPKA, JOHN STANIER
and IAN WILLIAMS

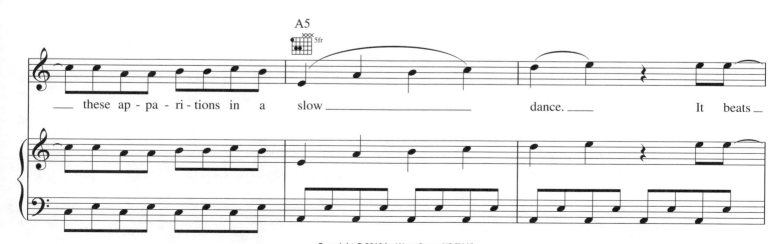

shot your - self. (...self, ...self, ...self, ...self,

...self, ...self, ...self, ...self...)

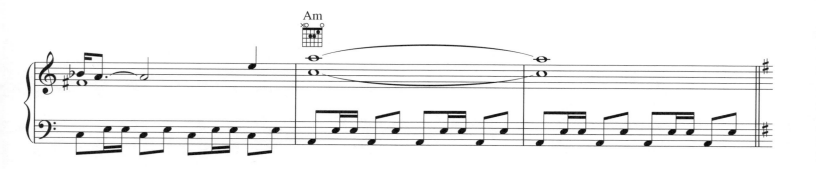

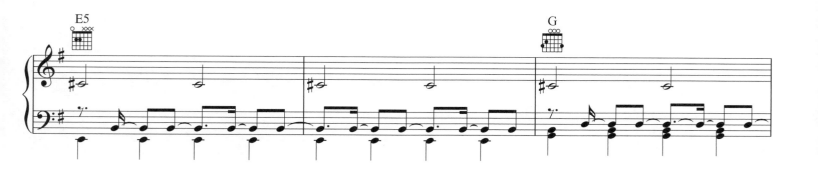

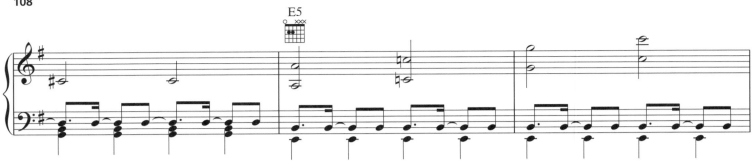

Fast, driving

Hey!   Hey!   Hey!   Hey!

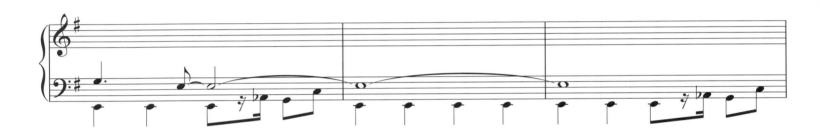

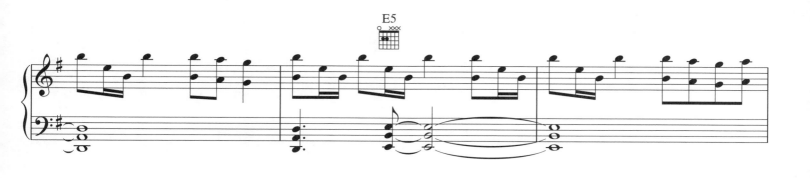

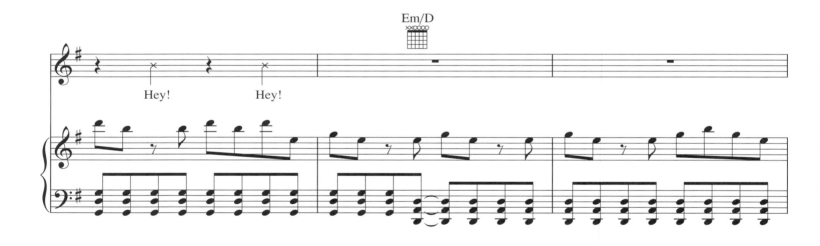

HOW CAN YOU SWALLOW SO MUCH SLEEP

Words and Music by
JACK STEADMAN

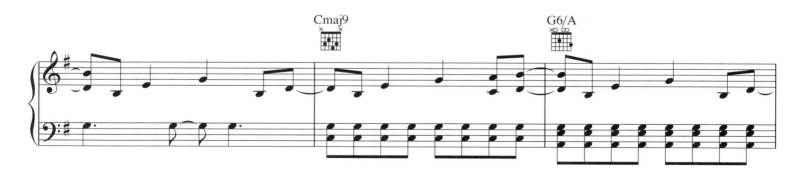

Is it late, is it late, is it late e - nough? There's a

wake you up? Is it late, is it late, is it late, is it late, is it

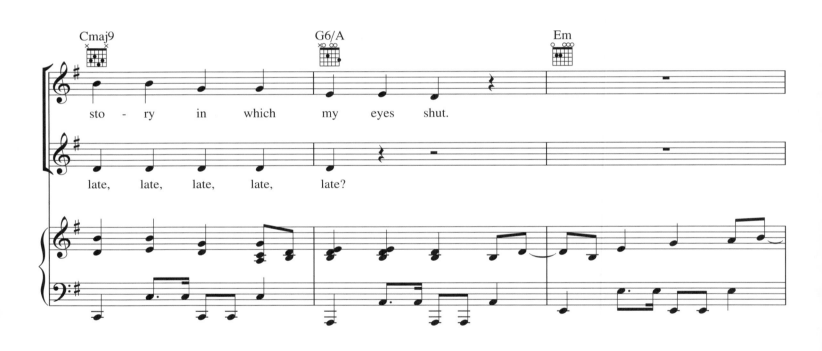

sto - ry in which my eyes shut.

late, late, late, late, late?

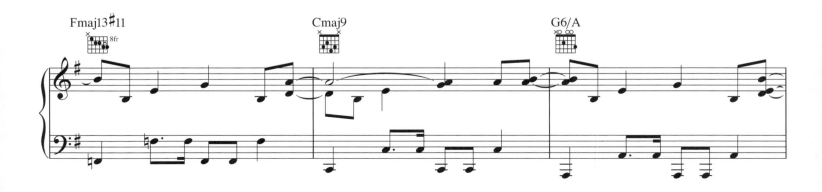

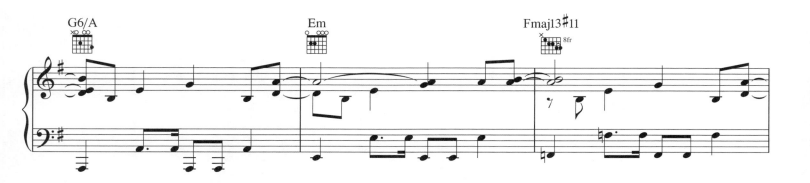